Boost Your Self-Confidence

CW00972803

SELF-CON]
PRACTICAL GUIDE TO THE
CONFIDENT YOU!

*One-Week Self-Confidence Challenge: 7 Days of
Challenges, Tips, and Workbook Questions to
Supercharge How You Live Your Life*

NATHAN BELLOW

WHY YOU SHOULD READ THIS BOOK

This book allows you to understand the only obstacle standing between you and your greater goals: your self-confidence level. Through an analysis of your past and the way you understand your present, you can begin to assess your current self-confidence levels and the very real changes you must make in your life to reach toward your goals and live a happier, healthier life.

With this book, you are offered a One-Week Confidence Challenge. Every morning, noon, and night, you are meant to assess a particular portion of your life on a very serious level. You are meant to answer questions in a notebook you've set aside as your "confidence notebook." As you put pen to paper, you can begin to realize the ways in which you can alter your actions and your emotions to fuel vibrancy and energy into each of your workdays, all your relationships, and your interior dialogue—or the words you say to yourself.

Do not wait another day to start the one-week confidence challenge. Assess yourself, answer questions, push yourself to do different, and new things, and bring quality and joie-de-vivre into your life.

At this end of this book, assess yourself with a state-of-the-art self-confidence assessment and understand how far you've grown. You'll be surprised how much confidence you can grow in yourself in just seven days. Supercharge your life. Supercharge your confidence instincts, and become the controller of your actions. You are wise; you are worthy of the life you are living. Make that life all it can be.

TABLE OF CONTENTS

CHAPTER 1. SELF CONFIDENCE: THE CENTRAL THEME FOR MAXIMIZING YOUR LIFE GOALS

CHAPTER 2. UNDERSTANDING YOUR LACK OF SELF-CONFIDENCE: PUSHING BACK AGAINST YOUR PAST

CHAPTER 3. ANALYZING YOUR SELF-CONFIDENCE LEVELS: HOW LOW DID YOU GO?CHAPTER 3.

CHAPTER 4. PREPARING FOR THE 1-WEEK CONFIDENCE CHALLENGE: UNDERSTANDING THE IMPORTANCE OF NEURAL-LINGUISTIC PROGRAMMING

CHAPTER 5. WORKBOOK CREATION AND MORNING, NOON, AND NIGHT OF YOUR FIRST SELF-CONFIDENCE CHARGED DAY: WORKING TO GAIN SELF-CONFIDENCE IN ONE WEEK

CHAPTER 6. MORNING, NOON, AND NIGHT OF DAY 2: 1-WEEK CONFIDENCE CHALLENGE

CHAPTER 7. MORNING, NOON, AND NIGHT OF DAY 3: 1-WEEK CONFIDENCE CHALLENGE

CHAPTER 8. MORNING, NOON, AND NIGHT OF DAY 4: 1-WEEK CONFIDNECE CHALLENGE

CHAPTER 9. MORNING, NOON, AND NIGHT OF DAY 5: 1-WEEK CONFIDENCE CHALLENGE

CHAPTER 10. MORNING, NOON, AND NIGHT OF DAY 6: 1-WEEK CONFIDENCE CHALLENGE

CHAPTER 11. DAY 7: YOUR FINAL DAY AND A SELF-CONFIDENCE ASSESSMENT: HOW FAR YOU'VE COME ABOUT THE AUTHOR

Chapter 1. Self Confidence: The Central Theme for Maximizing Your Life Goals

Ask yourself: how can you fuel yourself to move forward, to reach toward your goals, and find self-actualization in your life? How can you affirm your worth to your potential employers, your teachers, and your already self-confident peers?

That's right: you, yourself, must manipulate your own self-confidence.

Everyone aspires to work with someone who is self-confident. Every employer hopes to hire someone with self-confidence. Every parent yearns to fuel children with self-confidence.

When you're rich with self-confidence, you can boost yourself in the work world. You can live well with other rich, vibrant, self-confident friends by yours side. You can maintain equal relationships with employers rather than living in fear that they won't appreciate you, wont' like you.

You can accept yourself on a brand new level: you can accept that you deserve things. That you are worth it. That you should live in this world as an essential member rather than a passer-by.

And this book will help fuel you with the confidence to

succeed.

WHAT IS SELF CONFIDENCE?

But what is this "self-confidence" concept?

Essentially, self-confidence is the overall attitude people have about their lives and their actions. This feeling, this attitude allows you to hold positivity alongside a very essential sense of reality. Therefore, you can see the very best of every scenario without losing the context, the reality of the situation. You can only trust your abilities and your control of your life to a pinnacle, to a point. After that, you understand that your abilities limit you from ultimate success.

For example, your abilities might limit you from playing basketball. You can't quite jump as high; you can't quite improve your reflexes in order to catch the basketball "on a dime."

However, your abilities DO allow you to publish articles in the local paper. Your abilities DO allow you to communicate fluidly and easily when in interview-realm, ready and willing to push yourself for the story, for the proper angle.

Your personal abilities fuel themselves in specific areas of your life, and you are content with that, if you have self-confidence. You understand what you are good at, and you use that understanding to build yourself up in your surrounding world. Furthermore, you understand what you're not-so-good at, and you don't try to kill yourself on the basketball court.

Therefore, your lack of ability in one area does not affect your overall "mission" in the world. You understand your purpose, your goals, and you have the abilities to reach them. You expect to feel respect from your peers for your abilities and goals, and you therefore lend your own respect to your peers for their goals. Furthermore, you maintain a sense of humor. You don't feel the weight of the world; rather, you attain your goals without the undue stress that afflicts the majority of people. Even with your lack of stress, you are hardworking and dependable. You don't have negative stress pushing you to succeed; you simply have a drive to succeed for yourself, for the betterment of your personal goals.

WHERE DOES YOUR SELF-CONFIDENCE COME FROM?

You attained your current level of self-confidence and self-esteem at a very early age. Your childhood experiences and the way you remember those experiences readily influenced the way you thought about yourself. You'll begin to understand the ways in which these childhood experiences create poor self-confidence in the next chapter.

Luckily, you can drive forward from these past experiences to formulate new ideas of self-confidence, of self-worth. Note that in order to create new self-confidence, you must adopt brand new behaviors—all lined out for you in a 1-week challenge.

Your brand-new behaviors must affirm your belief in yourself; they must be action-oriented, ready to charge signals to your brain that you have worth, that you have value.

Remember that self-confidence is all about assuring your interior self that your exterior self has value. Treat your inside and your outside well in order to relate to your brain that you should exist in this world, alongside everyone else.

LINK ACTION AND BELIEF

Remember this: the perception you currently have of yourself is your essential belief-structure. If you feel that you're incapable, your self-confidence levels are continually plummeting until you find a way to understand your capabilities.

Fortunately, your actions can actually alter your beliefs. If you act like someone who is self-confident; if you radiate self-confidence through all you do and say, your actions will begin to feed your perception of yourself. You can alter your interior belief-system and begin to feel like a self-confident person on the inside. This will allow you to reach toward your goals, toward a more zealous sense of self.

Look to the behaviors of a self-confident person and begin to match what they do. Even if your interior self is a little "off" and lacking in self-confidence, you can begin to carry a different posture, a different manner. When your manner aligns with that of a self-confident person, you can feed a better interior sense of self.

4 CURRENT BEHAVIORS OF A SELF-CONFIDENT PERSON: UNDERSTAND HOW TO MATCH THEM

You recognize and understand which people in your life are self-confident. Look at them and try to understand them on a different level. Remember that they are not naturally self-confident. Rather, they have bad days and good days, just like you do. However, it's best to continually remember that they can find essential alterations in their unhappiness on their bad days in order to fuel ready energy into their lives.

Look to the following behaviors to begin to assimilate these behaviors into your own life.

1. THEY SPEAK WITH POSITIVITY DURING EVERY CONVERSATION.

During normal conversation, how often do you switch from happy hello's to dismal complaints about your life, what you have to do, and the rainy weather? Self-confident people do not slide from positivity. Instead, they discuss their lives with joy and engagement while asking positive-oriented questions of their conversation partner.

2. THEY TAKE COMPLIMENTS WELL.

Every time you receive a compliment, you sidestep it, don't you? You aren't willing to take the compliment, and you deflect it. These self-confident people hear expressions of interest, of honor from their peers, and they don't refute them. Instead, they are gracious and accepting. They understand the joys of giving, and they allow their peers to receive that joy of giving by accepting the gift of a compliment. The self-confident people show complete appreciation.

3. THEY DON'T SELF-PROMOTE THEMSELVES.

Occasionally, do you brag about yourself in order to feel like others approve of you? Self-confident people don't feel the need to do this. Instead, they hold complete modesty and do not feel the intense desire to bring attention to themselves. If you find yourself bragging often, you probably feel that you don't deserve respect without calling out for it.

4. EVERYTHING THEY DO PROJECTS THEIR INNER SELF-CONFIDENCE.

When you meet people on the street, you know if they're self-confident. They always greet you with smiles and eye contact. Their posture is confident and tall, and his body language initiates his ready self-confidence. Think about how you, yourself, talks and walks. Think about how you greet people. Everything you do either translates your self-confidence of lack of esteem.

RETAIN POSITIVE ACTION

Remember, last of all, they don't allow their doubts to penetrate what they want in their lives. People with self-confidence don't linger on their low-level beliefs on themselves, the beliefs that allow them to doubt their actions. Instead, they take positive action. They produce things. They affirm themselves with the understanding that they can do whatever they want. They create solutions rather than linger on the problems.

CHAPTER 2. UNDERSTANDING YOUR LACK OF SELF-CONFIDENCE: PUSHING BACK AGAINST YOUR PAST

Remember that your low self-confidence can develop in many places throughout your life. Because you are currently lingering in this low self-confidence realm, your low self-confidence is a large part of you; therefore, you might not be able to see it clearly.

This low self-confidence formulated itself in you at perhaps an early age, and your behavior began to affirm your belief that you were not good enough, that you didn't deserve respect from you peers.

CHILDHOOD-BASED REASONS FOR YOUR LOW SELF-CONFIDENCE

How did your low self-confidence formulate? How did it initiate itself in you and keep you from your true potential, from enriching human relationships, and your ultimate goals? Low self-confidence stems from many early personal events. The following reasons are the most common reasons for low self-confidence.

YOUR PARENT OR GUARDIAN WAS DISAPPROVING OF YOU OR YOUR ACTIONS.

Your first years were spent hearing that whatever you did wasn't good enough. The achievements you produced at school or in your personal life were always met with parent criticism. This excessive criticism leaves you feeling unconfident in your body; it leaves you with the shame of constant failure.

YOUR PARENT OR GUARDIAN WAS UNINVOLVED.

During your first years, you were particularly susceptible to your parent or caregiver's thoughts. You were aware when you did something to please them or when you did something entirely displeasing, like making a mess of the kitchen. However, if your parent was preoccupied or uninvolved with you as a child, you felt no desire or need to push yourself to achieve. When you did achieve something, your parent or caregiver gave no praise or no notice. Therefore, your achievement became unimportant to you because it held no light in your parent's eye. This initial feeling that everything you do doesn't matter can leave your adult self with the feeling that you are not accountable and that no one cares about you. You can feel unrecognized, disrespected. Oftentimes, if you have these carryover feelings from your past, you apologize for everything you do, even if that thing is good.

YOUR PARENTS WERE CONSTANTLY FIGHTING.

If your parents often fought when you were a child, you may have absorbed the negative emotions of your household. Oftentimes, children feel overwhelmed, like they caused the conflict and the disturbance between their parents. If this happened to you, you may carry the feeling of being tainted, like everything you touch, everything you involve yourself in becomes scarred.

YOU WERE BULLIED, AND YOUR PARENTS WERE UNSUPPORTIVE OF YOU.

If you were bullied and you had unsupportive parents, you are plagued with a lack of self-confidence. You felt unsafe outside of your home environment only to return to a home without support, without love. You felt hopeless in your everyday life, and you brought these feelings into your adult life. You sense predators in all the people you meet, and you tend to feel that anyone who befriends you is doing you a favor.

YOU WERE BULLIED, AND YOUR PARENTS WERE OVER-SUPPORTIVE.

It seems bizarre to link a lack of self-confidence and over-supportive parents. However, if you were bullied in school and you were met with parents who tried to hide you from the terrors of the world, you may be unprepared to handle the greater world as an adult. You were unable to develop an outer layer of protection. Therefore, when you try to embark into the world, you feel ill-prepared. Furthermore, your feeling of lack of preparation is shameful to you, leaving you to retreat back to familiarity in your parent's home. You feel your parent's high opinion of you; however, you understand that you just don't fit in the exterior world. Therefore, you feel an interior conflict between these two viewpoints. You feel that you aren't good enough to face anything that you don't already understand.

YOU WERE BULLIED, AND YOUR PARENTS WERE UNINVOLVED IN YOUR LIFE.

If you were bullied only to return to a home without attention, without notice of your exterior problems, you felt shortchanged. You felt unsafe in your exterior world and unnoticed in your home life. This formed ideas of isolation in you, leaving you to feel that no one wanted to listen to your problems. No one wanted to give you advice. Your isolation may linger with you in your adult life, leaving you unable to talk out your problems because you don't feel like they're important to other people.

YOUR LIFE WAS FILLED WITH TRAUMA.

Drastic physical, emotional, or sexual abuse brings a deep sense of low self-confidence and lack of trust in your adult life. You were forced into a strange emotional or physical position as a child, and your adult self has difficulty trusting anyone else. You may blame yourself for your past trauma in order to try to understand the trauma better, in order to make it your own. You may view yourself as a shameful person, a person who deserved what you went through when you were younger. In your adult life, you may not feel worthy enough to reach toward your goals or have meaningful relationships with people.

THE MEDIA AFFECTED YOU IN A NEGATIVE WAY.

As a child, you felt you couldn't measure up against the images on magazines, on billboards. You were never as thin or as beautiful as those people. Unfortunately, those images were airbrushed, altered. The people displayed lacked realistic qualities. Unfortunately, this feeling of inadequacy meets you around every turn even in your adult life as the airbrushing epidemic worsens. Even if your ultimate lack of self-confidence stems from a different childhood dilemma, this feeling of inadequacy in the media strengthens your negative feelings.

YOU STRUGGLED IN SCHOOL AND YOU DIDN'T HAVE SUPPORTIVE PARENTAL BACKING.

Your school days were filled with ultimate confusion. You slipped further and further behind in your studies and felt that no one stepped in to accommodate you, to assist you with your academic endeavors. Therefore, you grew up feeling stupid or "less than." As an adult, you doubt yourself and your abilities. You don't share your own opinions because you feel that they are somehow defective or undefined. You feel ultimate shame in your intelligence abilities.

YOUR BELIEF SYSTEM STRUCTURED YOUR LOW SELF-CONFIDENCE.

Many belief systems peg you into a place of perpetual sin. As a child, you felt like you were continually doing wrong, that you never measured up. You felt eternal guilt and shame during worship, and this passed on to your everyday life. You continually feel disappointment at your inability to reach perfection.

The above unfortunate circumstances fueled low self-confidence in your life. Note that these experiences cannot and SHOULD not affect your entire life. You can eliminate their power if you take immediate action. You can eliminate your negative sense of self, and you can understand your history in a different context. None of the above reasons for low self-confidence was your fault.

Remember, further, that the people who affected your low self-confidence when you were a child were affected with low self-confidence, themselves. You do not need to retain your low self-confidence and pass your self-confidence levels onto your children, your peers. You can stop the cycle.

Everyone holds his own path to feel safe, to feel self-confidence in his everyday life. Your path to find joy and forgiveness for both yourself and your past is different than anyone else's. However, you must try as best as you can to rid yourself of your life discomfort in order to find infinite self-confidence and self-affirmation.

CHAPTER 3. ANALYZING YOUR SELF-CONFIDENCE LEVELS: HOW LOW DID YOU GO?

Remember: your current level of low self-confidence is pushing you away from your goals and your ultimate desires for your life. As you learned in the previous chapter, your past has created this current feeling about yourself. Therefore, you understand that you must begin to act more confidently to alter your interior beliefs.

In order to boost your current levels of low self-confidence and low self-esteem, you must create a self-inventory. You must treat yourself like a manager would treat his store. A manager would take inventory in order to avoid excess and make room for new things in his supply.

You know that you have far too much low self-esteem in your inventory. You need to clear out your low self-esteem to make room for interior growth. If you don't take self-inventory of yourself, you will carry the dead weight from your past along with you for the rest of your life. This dead weight will push you away from your goals; it will hurt your chances of success.

Furthermore, you need to create a better environment for yourself. Your current environment is one in which you feel a lack of self-confidence. Is this lack of self-confidence purely internal, or does it stem at all from a negative environment? A self-inventory will allow you to assess your personal situation.

ASK YOURSELF THE FOLLOWING QUESTIONS TO TAKE SELF-INVENTORY

Remember that you can only move forward to greater self-confidence when you have a good perception of your reality and your personal perception of yourself. Ask yourself the following questions to assess your life on this very personal level. Utilize this tool to shed yourself of your negativity.

Ask yourself the following questions in order to assess your life on a very personal level. Answer the questions with complete truth. Remember, you can only move forward to self-confidence with a good perception of your reality, without the bad things you've been carrying around with you, and in a good environment.

HOW DO YOU GO ABOUT YOUR DAY: IN THE MORNING, AFTERNOON, AND EVENING?

Think about your daily routine. Think about how you wake up in the morning, what you usually have for breakfast, to whom you speak, how you get to work, and how you get home. Think about every action you make throughout the day and think about its direct result. Are you seeing the results you want out of your everyday life, or do you feel that your days are lacking something? Try to alter a few of your routines in order to produce different results. For example, if you feel like you're overweight, you could begin waking up a little bit early and going for a walk or a jog. Just this simple act of changing a bit of your routine could alter the rest of your day's actions.

DO YOU AFFECT OTHER PEOPLE IN YOUR LIFE IN A NEGATIVE OR POSITIVE MANNER?

Do you find that your actions or words negatively affect other people? Do you find that your actions—even if they come from a very deep, resentful place of low self-confidence—hurt your friends or family? Alternately, do you find that your actions promote others around you? Do you find that you are often building other people up with your words? Do people feel inspiration from you?

WHAT INSPIRES YOU?

Think about your life. What in your life gives you the strength to get up every morning? What has helped you come as far as you've come? What, for example, inspired you to read this book and work for better self-confidence? When you understand that, you can begin to nourish your inspiration and become even stronger.

WHAT, WOULD YOU SAY, IS GOOD ABOUT YOU?

So often you're told not to spout your own praises. This is both true and false. As mentioned in chapter one, you shouldn't spout your own praises in order to receive praise from other people. This shows a lack of belief in your own abilities. However, understanding what you're good at on a personal level is incredibly important. Ask yourself: what is good about you? What would you say are your best, most personal strengths? Do you find yourself motivated by beautiful things? Are you creative? Do you have a love of mathematics? If you understand what your strengths are, you can push yourself down these particular areas in order to achieve your utmost success. You can paint a better picture of the person you are right now, rather than the person you were in the past. If you don't understand your strengths and only know your weaknesses, you will give yourself no real room to grow.

WHEN DO YOU FEEL MOST CENTERED? WHEN DO YOU FEEL MOST LIKE YOURSELF?

It's important to know when you feel most like

yourself. Think about the environment you're in when you feel that way, and try to replicate the scenarios. In order to feel completely self-confident, you'll want to feel like you're representing your very best self. Therefore, a knowledge of how to be your best self all the time is incredibly important. What kind of people are you around? Are they the sort of people that build you up or tear you down? Is the environment a place known to you or unknown?

WHAT PEOPLE IN YOUR LIFE DO YOU ADMIRE?

Thinking about whom you admire in your life allows you to understand the qualities he or she has and how, exactly, he or she utilizes those qualities. Now, think about how that person might think about you. What qualities would he or she say they admire in you? List them.

WHAT DO PEOPLE COME TO YOU FOR? WHAT DO YOU OFFER OTHER PEOPLE?

Think about yourself in the context of your peers. Everyone has something he's good at. Everyone is separate from everyone else in very specific ways. There's something that you have that is special, that brings people to you asking for assistance or advice. Think about it. Are you especially good at cooking? Are you a good writer? Do you have athletic skills? There's something that makes you completely you.

CREATE A SKETCH OF YOUR INTERIOR SELF

Write the answer to each of the above questions. Write these things you like about yourself; write these things that make you different from everyone else. If you understand the ways in which you're different from everyone else, you can begin to understand your unique place in the world, your unique personality. Create a scrapbook using personal photos, pictures of people you admire, and magazine clippings of what you like to do. You are creating a portrait of your "best self."

If you're having a bad day, pull out the self-inventory questions and remind yourself all the things you're good at and all the things people appreciate about you. You don't have to think negatively about a specific event that you couldn't control; you don't want something you could have controlled to have negative effects on your progress toward self-confidence. Therefore, when something bad happens, focus on all the positivity in your life. Bring your mind to a different realm of thought.

Update your self-inventory every few months. Alter your written notes about your best self and reassign pictures to your scrapbook. Because you're always changing and working toward a better self-confidence, a better feeling about yourself, your self-inventory will have changed. Watch your scrapbook change over a period of years and feel your confidence growing.

CHAPTER 4. PREPARING FOR THE 1-WEEK CONFIDENCE CHALLENGE: UNDERSTANDING THE IMPORTANCE OF NEURAL-LINGUISTIC PROGRAMMING

Take just one eventful week to renew yourself, to fuel yourself with self-confidence and ready self-esteem. Take one week to rev your engines and take off from the standstill in which you find yourself.

Remember: you're battling back against your past: the past that forced you down this road of low self-confidence. You're battling back against your interior voice: the voice that tells you that you are invalid, that you can't do anything. You're grabbing your sense of worth and taking small steps, every single day, to feel a renewed sense of power.

During this chapter, you'll learn about Neural-Linguistic Programming's technology in order to fuel Neural-Linguistic programming into day 1 of your 1-week challenge. Fuel yourself with vibrant self-confidence.

NEURO-LINGUISTIC PROGRAMMING AND SELF-CONFIDENCE

Neural-Linguistic Programming is a science that studies how you can experience excellence through analyzing the top people in each field to understand how confidence, excellent people think, feel, and act. Through this NLP science, it's understood that anyone can learn how to feel, how to think, and how to act like these people. Through this understanding, anyone can reach toward these personal success heights.

Neural-Linguistic Programming provides a link between how you think your interior thoughts, how you communicate on both a verbal and non-verbal landscape, and how you behave as a result of your emotions. Because you hold within you a wealth of neurology, you are constantly conveying interior thoughts with information about your environment. Because you are a communicative animal, you immediately bring that information to light utilizing linguistic sounds. You transfer perceptions and beliefs into words, into communication. The general, overall analysis of your growth into a human being with patterns, with both internal and external behaviors, describes your programming. Therefore, how you think illustrates the neural pathways; how you communicate illustrates the linguistic pathways; how you behave illustrates your interior programming. Neural-Linguistic Programming believes that if you can outline how these different pathways connect, you can understand precisely how you operate in your exterior, social interactions. You can analyze how self-confident people operate their particular mechanisms, and you can learn to match their operations. When you match these self-confident people's mannerisms, you are practicing a core belief of Neural-Linguistic Programming. You are modeling.

When you practice Neural-Linguistic Programming

techniques, you'll begin to observe humans in an entirely different way. You'll see different linguistic and behavioral patterns that alert you to people's inherent self-confidence or lack thereof. Understanding the ways in which these people communicate, however, will allow you to communicate more fruitfully with them. As you begin to diagnose how these people communicate, you'll have the ability to turn the conversation where you want it to go. For example, if the conversation is lingering on the negative side, you'll have the ability to ease the conversation toward a more positive light. As mentioned in previous chapters, self-confident individuals thrive on positivity; positive words shed more light on these feelings, thus rejuvenating them on an interior level. Your actions speak to your beliefs and strengthen them.

ALTER THE MEANING OF THE PAST: FIGHT BEYOND WHAT YOU UNDERSTOOD OF YOURSELF AND YOUR LIFE

A unique concept in Neural-Linguistic Programming is this idea of submodalities, or "mapping." Understand: you have a map of your current, personalized reality that is completely different than anyone else's map of his or her reality. This is because the way you perceive the world is completely different than the ways other people perceive this same world. You are complex in that the things that happened to you as a child altered you and formed you into who you are today, and these same things did not happen in the same, particular way to other people. You stored everything that ever happened to you with the use of your five senses. When you bring the same pattern of senses back into your mind, you can actually relive the experience. You can see the same visual patterns and colors; you can hear the same music; you can feel the same texture or smell the same smell.

In order to alter your reality and push back against things in your past that are breaking you down and forming low self-confidence in your present life, you can actually adjust the memory of these senses. You can change the meaning of the past by bringing new ideas down your neural pathways. When you offer your brain a better way to remember a past event, your brain will grasp at it. This aligns well with the idea of evolution: an organism will evolve for the betterment of itself, just as your neural pathways will reorganize their memories for a better, more fruitful interior life. With enough practice, you can train your brain to remember only the made-up understanding of an event rather than the past, actual event. You need to drop a past feeling of something in order to rejuvenate yourself and fuel yourself into a new beginning. In turn, this reduces your interior senses of stress, therefore giving your neural pathways a much-needed break. Stress from your past lingering in your neural pathways does nothing for you on a personal level or on a molecular level. Your brain will be happy to let everything go.

NEURAL-LINGUISTIC PROGRAMMING ANCHORING TECHNIQUE

You've probably heard the story of Pavlov's dogs. When researcher Pavlov went to feed his dogs, he noticed that his dogs already had spit and slime coming from their mouths in preparation for the meal they were about to ingest. Therefore, Pavlov understood that his dogs' digestive systems were anticipating the food.

Pavlov was interested in this conditioned idea that the dogs' interior digestive systems could begin to prepare for food without first eating. In order to explore this idea more readily, he began ringing a bell every time he gave the dogs their evening meal. The dogs began to associate the bell with the meal. After several days, Pavlov rang the bell but did not deliver the food. He saw, however, that the dogs were so conditioned to the bell ringing that their digestive systems had already begun to operate. Slobber was sliding from their mouths.

Anchoring is classical conditioning. When you anchor something, you associate one, completely different thing with a specific experience. In Pavlov's dogs' case, they associated the ringing bell with the experience of eating and feeling nourished.

The utilization of anchoring in Neural-Linguistic Programming is this: when you anchor an experience or a feeling with an item, you can bring the feeling or experience back to your mind readily when you have a physical representation of the anchor. You can utilize an anchor, for example, to make yourself feel how happy you were when you saw someone you hadn't seen for a very long time. You can squeeze your ear and think about how happy you were over and over. After a while, when you squeeze your ear, you'll feel that happiness once again without even trying. You can actually alter your current mood by traveling, via your anchor, to a different state of mind.

CHAPTER 5. WORKBOOK CREATION AND MORNING, NOON, AND NIGHT OF YOUR FIRST SELF-CONFIDENCE-CHARGED DAY: WORKING TO GAIN SELF-CONFIDENCE IN ONE WEEK

The few days before you embark into your 1-week confidence challenge, you must begin to calm yourself and formulate a good mental state. This mental state will help you attempt to "give your all" when formulating this self-confident routine. After all, through this following week, you're working to reach toward your goals and meet new people; you're working to maximize your life.

Remember that going into this, you must set realistic expectations for yourself. At the end of this one-week challenge, for example, you will still have negative thoughts. You will still exist in the same strain of your environment. Your parents will still criticize you; your job will still irritate you. However, after this program, the way you act and receive the information from your environment will be completely different. You will no longer feel low self-confidence moving forward. Instead, you'll handle each individual problem as a person with self-confidence. You'll see yourself as a valid part of society, worthy of everyone's respect.

Remember: perfection is not a viable option. It is

completely unattainable. However, if you remember to utilize these one-week's worth of stocked tips, your self-confidence will begin to blossom. Remember that this challenge is not a get-confident-quick scheme. Instead, it is a renewed way of life. You must re-dress the way you live, alter the way you think in order to maintain true change.

UTILIZING A WORKBOOK TO RECORD WHAT YOU'VE LEARNED

It's incredibly important to write down what you learn as you go along the following one-week challenge. After all: this way, you can record your different morning, noon, and night activities, and you can answer the questions formulated at the end of each section. You can go back and understand how far you've come as you work through the program.

MORNING: ENGAGE IN A POWERFUL VISUAL EXERCISE

This initial day of the one-week challenge fuels you to re-evaluate the sense you have for your future self. This technique is rooted in the neural-linguistic programming discussed in the previous chapter.

The exercise creates a different neural pathway in your mind and a different way to communicate your new neural understanding to yourself and to others. Therefore, it brings a connection between your neural and linguistic pathways, altering your ultimate behavior.

Furthermore, it's important that you do this in the morning of your first day. It creates this neural pathway early and it helps focus your mind as you work throughout the rest of your first day.

1. Find yourself a quiet, semi-dark area. Make sure you're completely alone.
2. Begin by assimilating yourself in a peaceful state. Inhale and exhale very slowly. Bring your heartbeat to a lull. Feel every part of your body.
3. When you feel peaceful, open your eyes and imagine a mirror sitting in front of you.
4. Inside the mirror, you see yourself. However, that image is a little bit different. That image is a self-confident, successful you. Imagine the "you" in this context. Imagine how this person walks, talks, and behaves in your usual settings. Are these behaviors different than your usual behaviors?
5. Next, place yourself in the immediate shoes of this person in the mirror. Imagine yourself as this confident "other" self. Feel yourself walking and talking just like this confident person.
6. When you feel this confidence churning inside of you, cross your middle and ring finger together and say a particular word. Say something like: "Strength," or "Confidence." The word can be anything. The word should align with this feeling of confidence, and it should pair with the cross of your fingers.
7. Repeat this process several times. As outlined in

the previous chapter, you are anchoring this feeling of confidence.

8. Throughout this first morning, remind yourself of this trigger several times. Imagine yourself as this "new and confident" person by crossing your fingers and saying your code word. Do this in various, safe locations first. Try it at the grocery store before you talk to the cashier, or try it before you talk to your spouse. It's only your first day with your anchor, but you can strengthen it in the days to come.

WHAT TO WRITE IN YOUR NOTEBOOK:

1. Write Down How You Felt When You Lived the Life of the Person in the Mirror.
2. Write down how your feelings about yourself and your anchor are going to inform the rest of your day. Describe one instance during the following first day in which you affirm that you WILL utilize what you learned from "walking and talking" like the person in the mirror.

NOON: ANCHOR CONFIDENCE IN A SONG

Why do we listen to music?

Well: for one. Music is pulsing with infinite amounts of feeling. You probably have a song that pumps you up: a song that makes you feel like you're on top of the world. The music can be from any genre, in any language. This song is already a sort of anchor in your life—like the anchor you just formulated—in that it allows you to feel better than you normally feel. However, you must strengthen this anchor.

Examples of excellent confidence-boosting songs are:

1. Lose Yourself by Eminem
2. Stronger by Kanye West featuring Daft Punk
3. Eye of the Tiger by Survivor

During your lunch break, or sometime around noon, you can supercharge yourself by listening to a confidence-boosting song of your choice. As you listen to this song—on your iPod, in your car—imagine yourself as this more confident person. Listen to the song as many times as you want to, and get really into it. Clap your hands. Smile. Laugh. All of these exterior actions will inform your interior self.

Later, after your lunch break, or when you're on your way home from work—when you feel a little uneasy or a little strange—listen to this song. Remember the good feelings you had when you listened to this song at noon. Later, you can ANCHOR this song so that you can utilize it to feel better and more confident in any scenario.

WHAT TO WRITE IN YOUR NOTEBOOK:

1. What song did you choose and why did you choose it?
2. How does this song make you feel when you're happy?
3. How does this song make you feel when you're not-so-happy and feeling low confidence levels?

NIGHT: TRANSFER YOUR LEAST FAVORITE MEMORY INTO A POSITIVE ENCOUNTER

This one is an important nighttime routine. After all: how many times have you laid in bed, rolling around, hoping to eliminate your bad memories and just SLEEP?

Bad memories tend to haunt people and alter their futures. Your bad memories, for example, inhibit you from living to your full potential. You remember something terrible that happened last time you tried a particular thing, and now you are wary of trying that thing again. This forms into a negative cycle.

For example, earlier today, when you met new people, you were unable to open up and create any sort of relationship. You were embarrassed. Therefore, in the wake of that incident, you could be afraid to meet new people because you feel that you will look silly, will be unable to form relationships, and will generally experience displeasure with yourself. Ultimately, this pattern leaves you no room to meet any new people or grow in new environments.

In order to break this cycle, you must change how you think about your past memory during this hour before you go to bed. This is outlined with Neural-Linguistic Programming.

1. Begin by visualizing the real memory. Remember it for everything it was—imagining the senses you felt when it happened, the things you saw.
2. Then, send the memory far back, away from your

vision. Close your eyes and watch the memory fall away from you like a boomerang.

3. When the memory comes back into your vision, the memory is the new memory with the different meaning. The memory finds two people simply trying to create a conversation and learning from the meeting. You understand that you were meant to meet that person in order to step up and fuel your conversational skills. Therefore, you alter the meaning of the at-first negative interaction.

4. Picture the original memory again and then swish it back to the "new" memory. Do this many times. After at least ten times of visualizing this memory running away from you, try to remember the event in your head. Your neural passageways have assimilated a new formation. You will begin to remember only the pleasant, educational event.

WHAT TO WRITE IN YOUR NOTEBOOK:

1. What memory did you choose to focus on remembering differently, and why?

2. What negative feelings did you originally derive from that memory?

3. What did you learn from analyzing that memory differently?

4. How are you going to think of the memory, now? What did you learn from the memory?

Chapter 6. Morning, Noon, and Night of Day 2: 1-Week Confidence Challenge

The first day was meant to create personalized techniques to hone your interior thoughts about yourself. This day allows you to work your techniques into your exterior environment. You will begin to focus on maximizing your relationships.

Friendships are tricky. At their core, friendships are essentially two separate worlds colliding together and deciding, despite all differences, they'd like to coincide with one another and learn more about the other.

What's more, the fact that anyone would want to coincide with YOU—you with all your self-doubt—seems insane. How can you improve your ability to create a social life, and how can you hold the confidence to maintain strong social interactions? The following day will allow you to focus on these ideas.

When you succeed in creating human friendships, you'll learn that friendships are key boosts to your self-esteem in countless ways.

1. They help you make better decisions by giving you key advice for your tricky choices.
2. They walk alongside you and see things from your perspective.
3. They cheer you on when you succeed, and they comfort you when you fail.

Boost Your Self-Confidence

4. You don't have to go it alone when you have good friends by your side.

But how, exactly, do you form these initial, fruitful relationships?

MORNING: STRIKE UP A CONVERSATION AND SPEAK SLOWLY

Remember, in order for people to take you seriously, you must illustrate your confident sense of self. Sure, you haven't gotten to the end of the week yet; you haven't renewed your complete sense of self-confidence.

Remember, however: you can fake it. And, as mentioned before, faking confidence renews your belief in yourself on an internal level. Every little thing adds up.

1. In the morning: when you're on the train, arriving to the office, or simply in the line at the coffeehouse, strike up a conversation with someone you've hardly spoken to before.
2. If you have to, play your pump-up song from the previous day to prepare you to stretch yourself to speak to this new individual.
3. Also, remember to speak slowly, illustrating your authority. After all, a person with authority shows their sense of confidence, shows the fact that they are worthy to speak to.
4. Don't overdo it; however, slowing your regular, quick voice a few notches will boost your assuredness while talking to this new person. This new person will perceive you as someone he

should continue talking to.

WHAT TO WRITE IN YOUR NOTEBOOK:

1. Who did you decide to speak to, and why?
2. What did you ask them, and how did your tone illustrate who you were, what you knew, and what your mood was?
3. How did they respond? What was their body language?
4. Did you learn anything from your conversation you can take with you?

NOON: SEEK SOMEONE WHO CAN EMPOWER YOU WITH KNOWLEDGE

Remember: knowledge is power.

And fueling yourself with knowledge is one of the quickest strategies to begin feeling those waves of self-confidence. When you understand a new concept or learn a new fact, you are immediately boosted into a different world. Your environment alters.

Of course, you can empower yourself with this knowledge via the Internet at your noon lunch break. However, receiving knowledge from someone you seek out is much better.

1. Call an acquaintance on the phone—someone you know has knowledge about something you don't. Talk to him or her during your lunch hour, and enrich yourself for your hours ahead. This fresh

perspective will give you renewed insight.

2. Alternately, approach someone at lunch. Remember that his perspective on life is completely different than yours; therefore, your life-knowledge is completely different than his.

3. Swap knowledge and give each other pieces of each other's worlds. The person you approach will love discussing the knowledge he already has; he'll love speaking about himself and his world.

4. Remember, because you sought him out, he'll have a deep interest in what you have to say, as well. Open your eyes to the possibilities of knowledge.

What to Write in Your Notebook:

1. Who did you decide to call or seek out, and why?
2. How did you open the conversation? What questions did you utilize?
3. Did you speak slowly during the conversation? Did you smile? Did you laugh?
4. How did that person respond to you when you spoke?
5. Do you feel like you got enriching information from the conversation?
6. Do you feel like you offered enriching information to the conversation?

Night: Find An Exercise Buddy

Exercising fuels empowerment, and empowerment creates boundless self-confidence.

41

1. Ask an exercise-affluent person to go for a run or a walk with you this evening after work.
2. Note: you're including him in something he already enjoys: exercise.
3. Ask his exercise advice and tell him—in an incredibly positive manner—that you're hoping to get better in shape.
4. Other people feel the joy emanating off of you when you make a decision to better yourself. Simply including them on your exercise journey will form a bond between you.

WHAT TO WRITE IN YOUR NOTEBOOK:

1. Who did you choose to exercise with, and why?
2. How did you feel before you began exercising?
3. How did you feel while you were exercising?
4. How did you feel after exercising?
5. Do you feel like exercising (with or without this person) could enrich your life and fuel you with more self-confidence?

CHAPTER 7. MORNING, NOON, AND NIGHT OF DAY 3: 1-WEEK CONFIDENCE CHALLENGE

The first two days of this one-week challenge helped you to:

1. Focus on your internal self.
2. Eliminate negative thinking about your past.
3. Learn to formulate better person-to-person relationships

The following day will fuel insight on how to be present in any romantic endeavors. Remember: each moment of this specific day depends on your current relationship status: if you're married or if you're single.

If you're single, the following romantically-charged day will give you the confidence to approach people you already feel romantic toward or, perhaps, simply people you meet at random in your everyday life. Even if these approaches lead to absolutely nowhere, it's time you begin making a commitment to yourself and understand that you are good enough and well enough to have a romantic relationship.

IF YOU'RE MARRIED...

If you're married or in a serious, committed relationship, you and your partner might have serious problems because you have a low level of self-confidence.

1. Your past few years may have found you leaning heavily on this relationship as an unfair source of acceptance.
2. You may have brought your insecurities into the relationship, bringing ideas that you aren't good enough for anything outside the relationship. These feelings may translate into the relationship.

For example, if something negative happens at work or at school, you may expect your partner to see you differently, to actively see your value declining. After a while, you may begin to devalue your partner. You may begin to contaminate him or her in your eyes, telling yourself that you don't require a partner anyway.

You must begin to restore this very real human

relationship that has the potential strength to work you through every rough day—to work you through your low self-confidence to a better future. Your romantic relationships have true value when you enlist your energy to give them power.

MORNING: MEDITATE ABOUT A PAST OR CURRENT RELATIONSHIP

When you wake up in the morning, go to your quiet, meditative ground and ask yourself some personal questions.

If you're in a relationship, ask yourself:

1. How have you allowed the current relationship you're in to falter and fizzle?
2. Can you see actual instances in your mind that formed this negative blood between the two of you?
3. Do you feel your voice of self-doubt and low self-esteem working inside of you, altering the way you feel about your relationship without merit?

IF YOU'RE NOT CURRENTLY IN A RELATIONSHIP, ASK YOURSELF:

1. Have these negative, low self-confidence thoughts killed past relationships?
2. Are these negative thoughts altering your ability to meet anyone new?

You must acknowledge the actual reason behind your

faltering relationships or lack of relationships on an interior level. Only when you acknowledge these low beliefs in yourself can you rid yourself of them.

As outlined above in the Neural-Linguistic Programming section, you must picture yourself as a happier, more communicative person in a committed relationship. Spin your current thoughts of yourself into this thought and feel the way that happy, committed person feels. This committed feeling is your ultimate goal.

WHAT TO WRITE IN YOUR NOTEBOOK:

1. Answer the above questions: have your negative, low self-confidence thoughts killed any past relationships? Are these thoughts altering your ability to meet anyone new?
2. If you're married or in a relationship, answer the above relationship-oriented questions in your notebook.
3. Work to analyze how you can alter the current state of things as you record them in your notebook.

NOON: WORK TO MAKE EYE CONTACT

At around noon, you should work to have lunch with your romantic partner. Alternately, you should work to see a potential romantic partner—someone you have feelings for.

When you see him or her, you must focus on making continued eye contact when you are speaking. You must

46

make yourself seem open and positive, ready to listen to anything that person has to say.

Now that you understand that your lack of self-confidence is putting a gap between the two of you, you can "act" your way out of low self-esteem. Remember that your exterior actions alter your interior beliefs.

Furthermore, if you act confidently, your romantic partner will feel that you are up to the challenge of being in a romantic, committed relationship. You will seem sure of yourself and ready to take on a future with that person, regardless of either of your faults.

WHAT TO WRITE IN YOUR NOTEBOOK:

1. How did you feel when you exhibited complete eye contact when speaking to your romantic partner (or potential partner)?
2. How do you feel this eye contact altered the conversation?
3. Did the person with whom you were speaking maintain eye contact the entire time, as well?

NIGHT: LEARN THE VALUE OF TOUCH

Creating physical affection can go a long way in a relationship. Just feeling a small touch on your hand, on your elbow can bring endorphins to your brain, thus annihilating signs of stress.

Unfortunately, you cannot actually ask for a touch on this road to self-confidence. Instead, you must be the provider of this touch. You must be the action-oriented person in this scenario to illustrate your depth of self-confidence.

If you have a spouse or a partner, remember to keep this touch in mind. Your relationship may be on the rocks due to your low self-confidence and lack of ability to love yourself. If you feel that you're unworthy of love, you may have been curling away from your partner, skipping out on this one big category.

1. When you see your partner during this evening time, touch him or her on the shoulder.
2. Kiss them on the cheek or on the mouth.
3. Let them know, through pure physical actions, that you appreciate their existence.
4. They'll begin to return this gesture of touch, showing signs of appreciation as well.

If you don't have a partner, this "touch" concept is still inclusive. In Europe, when people meet one another, they give each other two kisses: one on each cheek. You don't need to go this far. However, during this evening, you should see someone you have feelings for and reach across and shake his or her hand.

Do physical things like opening the door for him or her or taking his or her coat. You don't have to physically touch him or her to give the idea that you're physically "there" for them. However, you must stop closing yourself off.

What to Write in Your Notebook:

1. How did you feel when you touched your romantic partner?

2. Did you feel like the touch altered your conversation in any way or created a different vibe in the room?
3. Did the person return any touch at any point during the rest of the evening?

Chapter 8. Morning, Noon, and Night of Day 4: 1-Week Confidence Challenge

This fourth day focuses on your work or school challenges in order to affirm your worth at these professional institutions.

Many people's overarching goals are fueled for work or school initiatives. And it's true that low self-confidence at these work places or schools can leave you feeling anxious. Although you've already been hired and already made it to your desired work or school, you can suddenly feel like you don't belong—which is never a good feeling.

Your school or your workplace is, on so many levels, your identity. You must reaffirm your self-confidence in these environments in order to take a true stance in your life. Your workplace is your livelihood; it is the source of many of your relationships and approximately forty hours of your week. Your school life is the stepping-stone to your livelihood. It is, furthermore, the source of your relationships and so much of your time. Therefore, in order to maximize your life, you must maximize your time spent at these places.

Morning: Write Down the Reasons You're at this Work or School

1. When you wake up before work or school on this

day 4, assemble a list of the reasons you were chosen to attend this school or be an employee at this workplace.

2. This list must be specific. For example, in order to attend this university, write that you achieved all A's in high school. In order to be hired as an employee at your company, write that you had to rock the interview process and graduate from a university.

3. List your accomplishments and your skills—the skills people see in you at work or school every single day.

By listing your skills, you'll stray your mind from your current panic-stance at your work or school place. You'll reaffirm your work or school identity.

WHAT TO WRITE IN YOUR NOTEBOOK:

1. Write the list of skills, as aforementioned above.
2. Write down how you feel you deserved to be treated at this workplace or school as a result of your skills.
3. Write down how you should begin to act because you KNOW you have these skills.

NOON: REMEMBER THAT NO ASSIGNMENT IS OVERLY THREATENING

During this fourth day, you must be proactive about your thinking. During this noon hour, you've probably already been presented with certain at-work or at-school tasks that seem mighty scary. You might have to give a presentation later about what you've already done this day; alternately, you might have to write a quick article about what you learned from your school assignment. The low self-confident person inside of you may be screaming at these assignments with fear.

During this day 4, however, you must remember that your perception of the situation is almost 100% of your truth of the situation.

Therefore, you must alter your perception of this day.

1. Instead of thinking of the presentation—or other assignment—as a scary, terrible thing, think of it instead as a situation that allows you to demonstrate all the hard work you've been doing.
2. Try to work through this thought with your Neural-Linguistic Programming techniques.
3. Remember your last presentation. Is it forcing you to look to the future presentation with fear?
4. Try to remember the last, bad presentation as it was, and then flip it on its head. Remember it differently. Remember it, instead, as a learning experience.
5. When you drop the bad memory of presentations or tests, you can move forward to the next ones with a renewed sense of self.

WHAT TO WRITE IN YOUR NOTEBOOK:

1. Write what, at this noon hour, is forcing you to feel anxious and lacking in self-confidence.
2. Write why, you think, this particular thing is forcing you to feel anxious.

3. Analyze what, in your past, could be influencing these current anxious feelings.
4. Write yourself a step-by-step list of things you must do to complete the task at hand.
5. Write about how you feel once you complete the task successfully. Remember how you feel.

NIGHT: ADD A CHALLENGE TO SOMETHING YOU'VE ALREADY MASTERED

At work or school, you probably have something that you do very well without thinking about it. Everyone has something—their general purpose for being there, really. And sure: this particular activity makes you feel good when you do it.

However, it's important that you disallow this activity to remain stagnant. For example, if you're really good at presentations, you might begin to slough off on them because you think they're a sure thing. You're always going to be good at them. Therefore, why should you try to maximize your potential?

In order to build your self-confidence, you must be willing to accept new challenges. If you add new elements to your presentation game, for example, you'll find your self-confidence growing exponentially. Not only are you good at presentations; you're able to innovate your presentations and make them more complex. Your boss will be incredibly impressed.

WHAT TO WRITE IN YOUR NOTEBOOK:

On the evening of day 4, write the following answers:

1. What is something you're really good at, be it at work or at school?
2. Why are you good at it? What specific skills do you have that allow you to be the best at it?
3. Assess how you could be better at this particular thing by watching the absolute greatest—the people who are known to be very good at this specific activity. For example, watch people on Youtube you KNOW to be excellent at presentations. Note the differences between what you do and what they do, and attempt to be better.

Chapter 9. Morning, Noon, and Night of Day 5: 1-Week Confidence Challenge

The past four days have yielded direct affirmation of the reasons for your low self-confidence, and as a result, you have been able to work through these reasons on a personal level.

For example, you understand the ways in which Neural-Linguistic Programming can eliminate your fears of failure by helping you to understand your past on a different, more educational level.

54

This day five allows you to reach toward health and happiness.

MORNING: DRESS YOURSELF WELL

Remember: you can trick your interior mind by doing something different to your exterior body. And when you look the part of a successful person on the outside, you'll feel more like a successful person on the inside. If you don't wash your hair for a few days, you are giving a message to your interior self that you don't matter. Furthermore, you are delivering a message to your peers that you don't care what they think about you, as well. And everyone wants his or her opinions to be respected.

1. Therefore, on this day 5 morning before you leave your house, do something extra special to improve your look.
2. Try a new hairstyle; wear a different tie.
3. Spruce yourself up in a unique way. Any alteration gives assurance to the world that you do care about yourself, that you are looking for improvement.
4. You'll further assure the world that you're unafraid of trying new things. This confidence will affirm your interior beliefs.

WHAT TO WRITE IN YOUR NOTEBOOK:

1. How did you alter your look, and why did you choose that specific alteration?
2. How did you feel about yourself when you looked in the mirror?

3. How did you feel about yourself when you were walking down the street?
4. Did you feel like your conversations with people flowed differently? Did you feel more confident in your opinion? Did they treat you differently?

NOON: PAY CLOSE ATTENTION TO YOUR INTERIOR DIALOGUE

Remember: your interior dialogue is the voice in your head, constantly talking to yourself. You may have a voice in your head that continually tells you that you're not good enough, that you can't possibly succeed.

On this day five noon's hour, you must work to take charge of that interior dialogue. During your lunch break, go off by yourself and trace your thoughts very carefully. Whenever you feel a negative thought bleed through you, write the following things in your notebook:

1. Write three things you like about yourself. These three things can be physical or emotional. They can describe the ways in which you interact with people.
2. Remember that these affirmations to yourself are not anything you'll ever show anyone. Rather, they allow you to beat back against the negative voice in your head.
3. Every day from now on, write down three affirmations to boost positivity in your head.

NIGHT: BEGIN PRACTICING THE SKILLS YOU REQUIRE TO ACHIEVE YOUR GOAL

Everyone has goals. And when you understand the goals you wish to reach toward, you must begin to hone the skills you require to reach those goals. You can hone these skills during your off-hours, after work. After all: these are the hours that are your own, that allow you to work toward things you actually want for your life.

For example, if your goal is to go to graduate school after undergraduate school, you must begin amplifying your knowledge about your particular subject. After all, you're looking to charge forward with this knowledge and become a master of your field.

This "knowledge" applies to so many different disciplines and goals. If your goal is to lose weight, begin to educate yourself about caloric contents and the foods you must eat in order to lose weight. Understand how many calories you need to eat every day in order to maintain your weight, and learn what your deficit should be. Working toward any goal requires much research and organization. If you have the tools to proceed, you must begin backing up your actions with education.

What to Write in Your Notebook:

1. What is your goal?
2. What skills do you require to reach toward this goal?
3. How can you hone these skills each day to reach toward this goal?

4. Make a schedule for yourself, and don't stray away from it. Outline each of the following days: how you will work toward these goals with a specific item each evening.

Chapter 10. Morning, Noon, and Night of Day 6: 1-Week Confidence Challenge

On day six, you must begin to loop together all that you've learned in the past few days. This day is a Saturday, a non-work day for most people. However, it's essential that you don't fall away from your self-confidence mantras. Look to the following to supercharge your weekend and streamline into the next weekdays.

Morning: Make Early-Morning, Daily Affirmations

On the Saturday morning of day six, you must wake up a half hour before you normally do. Note that this should be before your kids are awake, before you walk the dog— before everything. Go to a cool, quiet place away from everyone else in your house. Close your eyes and focus on your breathing. Descend into a meditative state.

As you linger in the meditative state, feeling your entire body working as one, feeling your neural passageways communicating the stance of your body in its environment, begin telling yourself affirmations. Tell yourself:

1. You hold the power to greatness.
2. You are, and have always been, a self-confident

person.

Repeat these mantras to yourself, and add any that are specific to this day. For example, if you have a big exercise regime you want to work toward on this Saturday morning, focus on these mantras. If you have an artistic endeavor you want to do to further your skills, utilize these mantras. Repeat these mantras until they become engrained in your brain, ready for activation on your way to work.

WHAT TO WRITE IN YOUR NOTEBOOK:

1. Write down the place you had your first meditative session, what time of day you had it, and your comfort level on a range from 1-5 as you meditated.
2. Write down your mantras so that you can read over them throughout the day.
3. Write down how you feel post-mantra meditation session. Ask yourself how you want those feelings to inform your activities the rest of the day. When you understand your target goal for these mantras, you have a greater possibility of reaching your goals.

NOON: CLAIM AN OUTSIDE INTEREST— BEYOND YOUR FRIENDS OR ROMANTIC INTEREST

On day 6, on this Saturday, you should focus on something that is uniquely for yourself—something outside of your current relationship or your current friendship. This thing could be a hobby, an exercise routine, or anything that puts your mind in a different zone.

Note that this step is beneficial for your love life on a different level. If you begin to hone your life outside of your relationship, you will begin to feel that you have more to offer in your relationship life.

For example: if you take up basketball as a hobby outside of your relationship, you'll have interesting stories to tell your partner or potential partner about last night's game. You'll seem interesting and more vibrant in the relationship because you have an interesting exterior life. You are well-rounded and able to exist outside of the realms of your romantic interactions.

Therefore, on this noon-hour of day 6, take stock of your old hobbies or anything new you might want to try. Sign up for an exercise class, head over to the craft shop, or enroll in a painting course.

WHAT TO WRITE IN YOUR NOTEBOOK:

1. Write down the hobby or creative activity you decided to try.
2. Write down how you felt about this particular hobby while you were doing it.
3. Write down an interesting fact about the hobby—something that you can talk about in conversation later with your partner or potential partner in order to introduce the fact that you have a wide, vibrant life.

NIGHT: ELIMINATE TOXIC FRIENDS FROM YOUR LIFE

This is a heavy one—especially on a Saturday night. As you further your journey toward self-fulfillment and self-confidence, you must analyze your environment and reconsider precisely where your low self-esteem is coming from. Oftentimes, people find themselves in toxic relationships with negative friends. These friends tend to bring you down instead of fueling you with self-confidence. And these friends have to go.

Therefore, for day 6's evening, ask yourself who your true friends are. Go through your contact list on your cell phone and analyze each name and your past history. If you find a name that makes you feel a lack of self-confidence, you must immediately delete that name from your contact information. Deleting them doesn't mean that person is cut from your life forever. It simply means you're taking a conscious action to eliminate a toxic environment while you heal.

WHAT TO WRITE IN YOUR NOTEBOOK:

1. Write down a list of all of the people you usually see during any given week.
2. Next to these people, rate these people on a range of 1-10 based on the level of self-confidence you feel as a result of these people. This self-confidence can be how you feel when you think about them, how you feel when you talk to them, or how you feel immediately after you see them.

3. Try to decide, based on this rating system, if you should see these particular friends again. Try to limit how often you see the negative people in your life, and see if this limitation fuels greater self-confidence in your life.

CHAPTER 11: DAY 7: YOUR FINAL DAY AND A SELF-CONFIDENCE ASSESSMENT

You've made it. It's Sunday, and already, you feel the shadow of self-doubt and low self-esteem receding from you. You have affirmations: you are worth it. You are worthy of all the goals you have in your own life, right now. You are worthy of good relationships with friends; you are worthy of good romantic relationships. You are further worthy of just being with yourself, thinking positive, affirming thoughts.

 Now that you've reached the final day, it's essential to take final stock of how far you've come since your first day in the self-confidence program. Look to the following quiz to better assess your interior dialogue, your interior perception of yourself, and your greater idea of the direction in which you're heading.

As you take the following quiz, follow along and record your results in your notebook. This way, you can come back and retake the quiz at a later date and see how far you've come when you continually utilize all the tips and tricks to fuel greater self-confidence in this book.

HOW HIGH IS MY SELF-CONFIDENCE?

1. When I experience a new situation, I am comfortable and generally ease into it without stress.

A. Always.

B. Sometimes.
C. Never.

2. I usually do what I believe people want me to do rather than what I think is generally "right."

A. Never.
B. Sometimes.
C. Always.

3. I always try—even when I know other people would have stopped trying by now.

A. Always.
B. Sometimes.
C. Never.

4. I always reach the goals I want to achieve.

A. Always.
B. Sometimes.
C. Never.

5. After I jump over an obstacle, I think about what it took to conquer that particular roadblock. Therefore, I always learn from what I've done.

A. Always.
B. Sometimes.
C. Never.

6. Every time I face a particular dilemma, I always feel negative and hopeless.

A. Never.
B. Sometimes.
C. Always.

7. I get positive feedback from my peers for my hard work often.

A. Always.
B. Sometimes.
C. Never.

8. I have peers who have similar skills with great success, just like me.

A. Always.
B. Sometimes.
C. Never.

9. I have a sheer positivity and energy about my life.

A. Always.
B. Sometimes.
C. Never.

10. I always avoid difficult situations.

A. Never.
B. Sometimes.
C. Always.

ANALYZING YOUR RESULTS:

If you answered mostly A's, you have high self-confidence. You are vibrant and energized about your decisions and your goals moving forward. You hold a unique positivity, and you will find success in life.

If you answered mostly B's, you might be uncertain about your level of self-confidence—and that's okay. Remember to keep working through the seven day program in order to initiate better self-confidence. Remember to eat well, exercise, fuel yourself with knowledge about your particular goals, and keep reaching.

If you answered mostly C's, you have low self-confidence, and you need to keep working. Remember: you aren't a lost cause! No one is. You are very worthy of your abilities, of your place in life. Keep meditating and performing appropriate mantras. Continue to find reasons you love to be alive. Affirm yourself that you have a place—that you deserve to be heard. As long as you continue working on the self-confidence tips written in the previous chapters, you will reach toward a better, more self-confident personality.

IN CONCLUSION: KEEP STRETCHING

The past one-week challenge allowed you to build a firm ground of self-confidence. You now understand the ways your brain operates and how it reacts to certain situations. You understand how to negate some of those negative thoughts and gear them toward a more powerful positivity.

You achieved a small goal on a greater path to an ultimate goal. Keep this in mind as you move forward, and set small goals for yourself each day in order to build your self-confidence. Continue to stretch yourself and boost your skills. Do a little something every single day to push yourself. If you continue to work toward self-confidence, you'll actually earn the positive feelings you already feel. You'll earn these feelings and therefore find no reasons to refute them. They are yours. They are payment for your days of hard work.

Moving forward, it's important to remember to always act like a positive, self-confident person. Even when your life begins to crumble around the edges, you can charge toward your goals and bypass fallbacks with these honed techniques.

Remember not to give up on yourself. Remember that even the most self-confident individuals have low-confidence days. However, if you remember your goals, if you remember your powerful positivity, you'll have the ability to change everything.

ABOUT THE AUTHOR

My mission with this is to be able to help inspire and change the world, one reader at a time.

I want to provide the most amazing life tools that anyone can apply into their lives. It doesn't matter whether you have hit rock bottom in your life or your life is amazing and you want to keep taking it to another level.

If you are like me, then you are probably looking to become the best version of yourself. You are likely not to settle for an okay life. You want to live an extraordinary life. Not only to be filled within but also to contribute to society.

OTHER BOOKS BY NATHAN BELLOW

<u>Positive Psychology: A Practical Guide to Personal Transformation: Motivational Psychology: Gain Confidence in Every Area of Your Life (Applied Psychology)</u>

It doesn't matter where you are at in life. You may have an outstanding life and ready to take it to the next level or you may have hit rock bottom. Regardless of your situation, this book will help you.

This book will help you gain a new mindset about life and will improve your image as well as your perception of your self-worth. This happens through different aspects and circumstances in your life as detailed in a chapter-by-chapter guide that you can read. Later on, you can apply what you learn and make these life lessons your own. With this book, there is no other direction but towards your best self. By this handy personal-development reference, you will be able to comprehensively assess where you are right now and find ways to get to where you want to be in life.

<u>Leadership: Inspiring Others The Way The Legends Do</u>

This is for all the leaders out there who are set to make change. This is also for all those who are leaders in the making. We are going to change things, starting today.

This book is made for people who want a guide on how to discover their leadership traits, and it is made for people who want to discover what it means to become one. It is also to make readers understand that leadership in itself is a skill that is made up of many other skills. Luckily, it is something that can be learned through process, and this book would show you how.

Reading this book would also make you understand why great leaders of history became leaders. It will also show you how leadership in every part of society is actually part of the humanity's need for such people. Here, you can learn how to bring out the leader in you by assessing the situation, just like how all great leaders did.

Here Are Some Of The Things You'll Learn...

Why You Want to Become A Leader

How to Become the Leader that You Want

Making Decisions As a Leader

How To Win Friends

Bringing the Best in Others

Much, much more!

The Power of Affirmations: Improve The Quality of Your Life By Reprogramming Your Subconscious Mind: Affirmations Book for the Subconscious Mind

You're about to discover how to exponentially improve the quality of Your Life by taking control of your inner voice. Find out how your negative Thinking has kept YOU from living the Life that You Deserve. Researchers have concluded that those with a Positive Internal Dialogue have Higher rates of Success.

Here Are Some Of The Things You'll Learn...

What Are Positive Affirmations

How Positive Affirmations can Help Transform Your Life

Positive Affirmations for Confidence, Self-Esteem, Relationships, Career, and much more.

How to Make Affirmations a Habit

All The Techniques to Use For The Affirmations To Work For You

Much, much more!

One Last Thing...

If you enjoyed this book or found it useful I'd be very grateful if you'd post a short review on Amazon. Your support really does make a difference and I read all the reviews personally so I can get your feedback and make this book even better.

Thanks again for your support!

Printed in Great Britain
by Amazon

43105446R10045